First published by Living With Purpose Publishing, LLC
2026 Copyright © 2026 by JennaLynn Myers

First edition

ISBN: 979-8-9952744-6-9

A Note From the Author

Dear Reader,

This book was written to help you lean on God's Word, no matter what else is going on in your life.

There have been many moments over my lifetime, when I have been at a loss for words but knew I needed to pray and meditate on God's Word. My hope and prayer is that this book can be something you turn to during the many trials of motherhood. I hope these prayers and verses bring you comfort and closer to God.

Each of the verses I selected were done so with great intention and prayer. I do, however, highly recommend not only meditating on the individual verses, but also opening your Bible and reading the chapter they are a part of. It helps to have the full picture.

I chose a variety of biblical translations, as I feel some versions are more powerful given a particular focus. I encourage readers to look up the verses in the version they feel most comfortable with.

I also included a short section at the very end of this book to assist you in planning a vision for your family. Vision planning allows you to come together as a unit. It is important to pray together and to cultivate a home where communication is clear.

Above all, know God is with you, always. You do not need to be a perfect mom. You just need to carry out the will God has put on your heart.

With love,
Jenna

Table of Contents:

Prayers and Bible Verses for:

When you . . .

For throughout the year . . .

you are anxious

Lord,
I know anxiety and fear does not come
from you. I know it is the devil trying to
get a foothold and trying to distract me
from all the good in my life. I ask, Lord,
that you calm my heart and mind. I thank
you for my children and the role of being
their mother. I am thankful you have
equipped me to nurture and guide them. I
know that you will continue to equip me
if I seek and focus on you Lord. I am so
thankful that with you, I need not fear.
Lord, help me to focus on you and feel
your comfort.

Amen

Colossians 3:15
And let the peace that comes from Christ
rule in your hearts. For as members of one
body you are called to live in peace. And
always be thankful. (ESV)

1 Peter 5:7
Give all your worries and cares to God, for
he cares about you. (NLT)

Philippians 4:6
Do not be anxious about anything, but in
every situation, by prayer and petition,
with thanksgiving, present your requests
to God. (NIV)

John 14:27
"I am leaving you with a gift—peace of
mind and heart. And the peace I give is a
gift the world cannot give. So don't be
troubled or afraid." (NLT)

you are consumed with busyness

Lord,
I am struggling with filling my calendar. I feel uneasy with whitespace and feel the need to ensure I am busy in my own life and my children's. Sometimes I wear busyness as a badge of honor, but I know that is not what you desire for me Lord. Busyness is taking over my life Lord, and while I was seeking to fill my cup with good friends, activities, and other commitments, I know it is too much. I know, Lord, that the only thing that can truly fill my heart is you. Please help me to enjoy the life you have given me and to stop chasing things to make me feel whole, as only you can do that Lord. I thank you for the freedom to choose what is best for our family and I ask for your wisdom as I pair down our calendar and make wise choices.

Amen

you are consumed with busyness

Luke 10:41-42
But the Lord said to her, "My dear
Martha, you are worried and upset over all
these details! 42 There is only one thing
worth being concerned about. Mary has
discovered it, and it will not be taken
away from her." (NLT)
(encouraged to read chapter 38)

Psalm 127:1-2
It is useless for you to work so hard from
early morning until late at night,
anxiously working for food to eat;
for God gives rest to his loved ones.
(NLT)
(encouraged to read chapter 127)

Isaiah 58:13
"Keep the Sabbath day holy.
Don't pursue your own interests on that
day, but enjoy the Sabbath
and speak of it with delight as the
Lord's holy day. Honor the Sabbath in
everything you do on that day, and don't
follow your own desires or talk idly. (NLT)

you are consumed by Technology

Lord,
While I know a technological world is the world I'm raising my children in, I also know it has taken too much of our focus. Please help me to renew the wonders of your creation. Please help us not allow addictive and isolating behaviors to take a stronghold, but to spend time in your word, the outdoors, and together in fellowship. Help me to balance the ever-evolving world around us, with the simplicities you created for us to enjoy. Help us to use technology in a way that is pleasing to you and not an idol. Thank you for the benefits of today's world and for your wisdom navigating life filled with technology.

Amen

you are consumed by Technology

Hebrews 12:1-2
Therefore, since we are surrounded by so
great a cloud of witnesses, let us also lay
aside every weight, and sin which clings so
closely, and let us run with endurance the
race that is set before us, 2 looking to Jesus
(ESV)

Colossians 3:2
Set your minds on things that are above,
not on things that are on earth. (ESV)

Psalm 119:37
Turn away my eyes from looking at
worthless things,
And revive me in Your way. (NKJV)

1 Corinthians 10:13
The temptations in your life are no
different from what others experience.
And God is faithful. He will not allow the
temptation to be more than you can stand.
When you are tempted, he will show you a
way out so that you can endure. (NLT)

you are comparing

Lord,

I thank you for the unique way you made me and my children. I know you gave me my children for a reason and while I sometimes feel another mother could do things a better way, I know you have placed my children in my care because you know best. Lord, I ask you to calm my heart and focus my eyes on you and not on social media, my neighbors, or other moms around me. Help me to not compare my children to other children either, as mine were made perfectly in your image Lord. Help me to stay on the path you have laid out for our family and continue without wavering. Lord, I thank you for reminding me the grass is greener where I water it and I ask you to help me to remember that anytime I begin to question my worth and ability as a mother. I thank you for your love and peace.

Amen

Galatians 1:10
Am I now trying to win the approval of human beings, or of God? Or am I trying to please people? If I were still trying to please people, I would not be a servant of Christ. (NIV)

Galatians 6:4
Pay careful attention to your own work, for then you will get the satisfaction of a job well done, and you won't need to compare yourself to anyone else. (NLT)

1 Corinthians 12:7, 11, 18-21
A spiritual gift is given to each of us so we can help each other. 11 It is the one and only Spirit who distributes all these gifts. He alone decides which gift each person should have.
18But our bodies have many parts, and God has put each part just where he wants it. 19 How strange a body would be if it had only one part! 20 Yes, there are many parts, but only one body. 21 The eye can never say to the hand, "I don't need you." The head can't say to the feet, "I don't need you." (NLT)
(It is encouraged to read 1 Corinthians 12 in its entirety)

you are discontent

Lord,
I am feeling discontent. The world around me is constantly showing me what else is available and how things in my life don't measure up to all the latest and greatest. Lord, help me to remember that much of what I prayed earnestly for I now have. Help me to remember that while new things, a bigger home, toys and gadgets, and updated decor are not what fulfills us, only spending time with you and in your word can do that. Please help me to take a look around and list several things each day that I am thankful for. For I know a grateful heart, is a content heart.

Amen

you are discontent

Philippians 4:11-13
Not that I am speaking of being in need,
for I have learned, in whatever situation I
am, to be content. 12 I know how to be
brought low, and I know how to abound.
In any and every circumstance, I have
learned the secret of facing plenty and
hunger, abundance and need. 13 I can do all
things through him who strengthens me.
(ESV)

1 Timothy 6:6-8
But godliness with contentment is great
gain, 7 for we brought nothing into the
world, and[a] we cannot take anything out
of the world. 8 But if we have food and
clothing, with these we will be content.
(ESV)

you need community

Lord,

I am desperate for community and companionship. Motherhood can make me feel like I am on an island some days. I am longing for connection with other mothers and families. Please give me discernment when seeking out others. Please help me to be kind, have an open heart, and to share your love. Lord, it is hard to trust and tiring to put myself out there, but I ask for the fortitude to do so. Please place people in my children and I's lives that lift us up and do not drain us. Help us find community but also know when we should leave a table. Help us watch our words and help our relationships glorify you. Thank you, Lord, for your constant presence, even when I am feeling lonely.

Amen

you need community

Joshua 1:9
"Have I not commanded you? Be strong
and of good courage; do not be afraid, nor
be dismayed, for the Lord your God is
with you wherever you go." (NKJV)

Proverbs 13:20
Walk with the wise and become wise;
associate with fools and get in trouble.
(NLT)

Hebrews 10:24-25
And let us consider how to stir up one
another to love and good works, 25 not
neglecting to meet together, as is the habit
of some, but encouraging one another,
and all the more as you see the Day
drawing near. (ESV)

Proverbs 27:17
As iron sharpens iron,
so a friend sharpens a friend. (NLT)

you are feeling hurt by a friend

Lord,

Right now, my heart is hurting. I have been let down by another and the situation feels unkind. I thought I could confide in this friend and that we were closer than we actually are. Lord, I know we are all sinners and I ask that you help soften my heart toward this person. Please help me to show your love and forgiveness, but also give me discernment to move on from this relationship, if that is your will. Lord, I know not everyone is my life for the duration but maybe just a season and while this hurts deeply, I know you will ultimately use this for good. I am thankful you are always with me Lord and I know you will use this situation for good. Please help me to grow and become more like you through this challenging experience. Please surround me with those who truly love you Lord, and genuinely care for me.

Amen

Psalm 34:18
The Lord is near to the brokenhearted
and saves the crushed in spirit. (ESV)

Psalm 147:3
He heals the brokenhearted
and binds up their wounds. (NIV)

Colossians 3:13
Make allowance for each other's faults,
and forgive anyone who offends you.
Remember, the Lord forgave you, so you
must forgive others. (NLT)

Ephesians 4:29
Do not let any unwholesome talk come
out of your mouths, but only what is
helpful for building others up according
to their needs, that it may benefit those
who listen. (NIV)

Proverbs 16:28
A troublemaker plants seeds of strife;
gossip separates the best of friends.
(NLT)

Lord,

It is very easy for me to want to brag about my child. It is very tempting to let others know of all the accomplishments they've made, the books they have read, the activities they are in, and the success they've had. Lord, while sharing positive outcomes is not unbiblical, I know boasting and doing so without the right heart is a sin. Please help me to encourage others moms and share our success, while still remaining humble. For while this may feel like an easier season, I know that challenges in motherhood can come at anytime. Please help me to be humble and not haughty Lord. Thank you for helping me to become more like you through the peaks and valleys motherhood brings.

Amen

you lack humbleness

Psalm 25:9
He leads the humble in doing right,
teaching them his way.(NLT)

James 4:6
But he gives us more grace. That is why
Scripture says:
"God opposes the proud
but shows favor to the humble."
(NIV)

Ephesians 4:2
Always be humble and gentle. Be patient
with each other, making allowance for
each other's faults because of your love.
(NLT)

Romans 12:3
For by the grace given me I say to every
one of you: Do not think of yourself more
highly than you ought, but rather think of
yourself with sober judgment, in
accordance with the faith God has
distributed to each of you. (NIV)

you need motivation to keep mothering with intention

Lord,

I know you've called me to steward my children, but I am so tired. Lord, I feel frustrated and unsure if my efforts are worth it some days. I ask that you give me the strength and fortitude to move forward. I ask that you change my heart and calm my nerves, so we can move forward with joy. I ask that you equip me and guide me as a mother. I thank you blessing me with my particular children and I trust that you have put me in this position for a reason. I know your word says to not grow tired of doing what is right, so I ask you to equip me with strength and motivation to move forward. Thank you for always being in my corner Lord.

Amen

you need motivation to keep mothering with intention

Galatians 6:9-10
So let's not get tired of doing what is good. At just the right time we will reap a harvest of blessing if we don't give up. 10 Therefore, whenever we have the opportunity, we should do good to everyone—especially to those in the family of faith. (NLT)

1 Corinthians 15:58
So, my dear brothers and sisters, be strong and immovable. Always work enthusiastically for the Lord, for you know that nothing you do for the Lord is ever useless. (NLT)

2 Corinthians 12:9
But he said to me, "My grace is sufficient for you, for my power is made perfect in weakness." Therefore I will boast all the more gladly of my weaknesses, so that the power of Christ may rest upon me. (ESV)

you are tired & need sleep

Lord,

I am so tired and need rest so badly. I need your comfort and peace to fall asleep at night and to sleep soundly. I pray my children can sleep soundly and we all can awaken refreshed and joyful in the morning. I pray you will refresh my body and my soul Lord. That you will let me take the day as it comes and find moments of rest. Thank you, Lord, for your peace and your love. Thank you that I can rest in You Lord and know that you will equip me through this tiring stage. I thank you for the gift of rest, and I ask you to help me to find rest in you and in my schedule, so I do not burnout and so my children can have the best version of their mother. I thank you for the model of rest you have given us as a reminder that rest brings fruit and is necessary for us all.

Amen

you are tired & need sleep

Psalm 3:3-5
But you, O Lord, are a shield about me,
my glory, and the lifter of my head.
₄ I cried aloud to the Lord,
and he answered me from his holy hill.
Selah
₅ I lay down and slept;
I woke again, for the Lord sustained me.
(ESV)

Psalm 4:8
In peace I will lie down and sleep,
for you alone, O Lord, will keep me
safe. (NLT)

Proverbs 3:21-24
My son, do not let wisdom and
understanding out of your sight,
preserve sound judgment and
discretion;
₂₂ they will be life for you,
an ornament to grace your neck.
₂₃ Then you will go on your way in safety,
and your foot will not stumble.
₂₄ When you lie down, you will not be
afraid;
when you lie down, your sleep will be
sweet. (NIV)

you feel weary

Lord,
I'm feeling weary. I am physically and
emotionally worn out Lord. I feel the
weight of the world on my shoulders and
I feel I cannot get anything quite right.
Lord, I need help to get off this
rollercoaster of over productivity and
exhaustion. I need you to take my
burden Lord and to show me where I can
step back. I feel something needs to give,
but I do not see how it is possible right
now. I need to feel your presence and
comfort Lord. I need your wisdom and
discernment to help prioritize things that
must get done, but to not overextend
myself as I have been doing.
Thank you for hearing my cries and for
taking my burden. Thank you for making
it so I can rely on you Lord and not
myself.

Amen

you feel weary

Isaiah 40:31
But those who wait on the Lord
Shall renew their strength;
They shall mount up with wings like
eagles,
They shall run and not be weary,
They shall walk and not faint. (NKJV)

Matthew 11:28-29
Then Jesus said, "Come to me, all of you
who are weary and carry heavy burdens,
and I will give you rest. (NIV)

2 Corinthians 4:17-18
For this light momentary affliction is
preparing for us an eternal weight of glory
beyond all comparison, 18 as we look not to
the things that are seen but to the things
that are unseen. For the things that are
seen are transient, but the things that are
unseen are eternal. (ESV)

you are sick

Lord,
My body is weak and tired. It has been
overcome with illness. Lord, I need your
healing and your strength. I also need rest
and rejuvenation. Lord, I know you can
heal and that your word is health and
healing to my body. Please, Lord, wrap me
in your love and comfort. Give me rest.
Lord, I thank you for your protection and
healing. I thank you, that even though I
do not have the strength to complete my
daily tasks, I can seek strength and refuge
in you. I also know that we were called to
rest and I thank you for giving me the
opportunity to rest and care for the body
you have entrusted me.

Amen

you are sick

Psalm 103:2-3
Let all that I am praise the Lord;
may I never forget the good things he
does for me.
₃ He forgives all my sins
and heals all my diseases. (NLT)

Proverbs 4:20-22
My son, listen to my words. Turn your ear
to my sayings. ₂₁ Do not let them leave
your eyes. Keep them in the center of your
heart. ₂₂ For they are life to those who find
them, and healing to their whole body.
(NIV)

Psalm 41:3
the Lord sustains him on his sickbed;
in his illness you restore him to full
health. (ESV)

Matthew 11:28
[Then Jesus said,] "Come to me, all you
who are weary and burdened, and I will
give you rest." (NIV)

you feel guilt for taking time for yourself

Lord,

I have so many things to get done each day but one of those tasks I have been neglecting is caring for my body and heart. Please help me to not feel guilt for the quiet I need with you, for that is what will allow me to continue to be a loving and diligent mom. Please help me also to care for the body you have given me by moving and resting it as needed. Please help me to not feel guilt for taking moments for myself. I know doing so allows me to be healthier for my family, as a worn-out mom is not helpful to my family. Thank you for showing me that even Jesus needed rest and time with you. Help me to be a good example for my children in caring for myself in ways which glorify you.

Amen

you feel guilt for taking time for yourself

Luke 5:16
But Jesus often withdrew to lonely places and
prayed. (NIV)

Mark 6:31-32
And he said to them, "Come away by yourselves
to a desolate place and rest a while." For many
were coming and going, and they had no leisure
even to eat. 32 And they went away in the boat to
a desolate place by themselves. (ESV)

Mark 1:35
Before daybreak the next morning, Jesus got up
and went out to an isolated place to pray. (NLT)

1 Corinthians 6:19-20
Don't you realize that your body is the temple of
the Holy Spirit, who lives in you and was given
to you by God? You do not belong to yourself, 20
for God bought you with a high price. So you
must honor God with your body. (NLT)

your marriage is in need

Lord,

Motherhood consumes much of my time and energy and I have noticed I don't have much left over for my marriage. I know my marriage needs to come first but some days I feel worn out from meeting everyone's needs. I ask that you help my husband and I connect and spend time with you in prayer. I ask that you help me to let go of some of the tasks and commitments that take much of my energy and instead prioritize my marriage. I know it is best for our family unit to have you at the center and then to put our marriage next in line. Please guide my husband and I in how to make that happen. Help my heart to not be frustrated or resentful when I feel the load of motherhood is heavy and for my husband to also recognize the hard work I am putting in, inside our home. Thank you for my husband, Lord. Please bless our marriage and let it be one that honors you.

Amen

your marriage is in need

Ecclesiastes 4:9-12
Two are better than one,
because they have a good return for their labor:
10 If either of them falls down,
one can help the other up.
But pity anyone who falls
and has no one to help them up.
11 Also, if two lie down together, they will keep
warm. But how can one keep warm alone?
12 Though one may be overpowered,
two can defend themselves.
A cord of three strands is not quickly broken.
(NIV)

Ecclesiastes 9:9
Enjoy life with your wife, whom you love, all the
days of this meaningless life that God has given you
under the sun—all your meaningless days. For this
is your lot in life and in your toilsome labor under
the sun. (NIV)

Colossians 3:13-14
Make allowance for each other's faults, and forgive
anyone who offends you. Remember, the Lord
forgave you, so you must forgive others. 14 Above
all, clothe yourselves with love, which binds us all
together in perfect harmony. (NLT)

Lord,

I am so thankful for the gift of motherhood, but I am running low on patience. My temper is short and my words are not always kind, Lord. Please change my heart from one of frustration and irritation, to being softer and kinder. Help me to be slow to respond when I am feeling frustrated. I know a quick temper is not a quality that will make our days successful, so I ask that you help me to stop and focus on you in moments of frustration. Please help me to remember the grace you have given me and how my children deserve that same grace. You always welcome me with open arms Lord, and I want to do the same for my children. Help me to ask children for forgiveness when I am impatient and to take a moment to focus on you, so I can then focus on them with joy. Thank you for your grace.

Amen

you need patience

James 1:12
God blesses those who patiently endure testing
and temptation. Afterward they will receive the
crown of life that God has promised to those
who love him. (NLT)

James 1:19-20
My dear brothers and sisters, take note of this:
Everyone should be quick to listen, slow to
speak and slow to become angry, 20 because
human anger does not produce the
righteousness that God desires. (NIV)

Proverbs 16:32
Patience is better than power, and controlling
one's emotions, than capturing a city. (CSB)

Proverbs 15:18
A hot-tempered person starts fights;
a cool-tempered person stops them. (NLT)

Ecclesiastes 7:9
Control your temper,
for anger labels you a fool. (NLT)

you are raising a special needs child

Lord,

I am so thankful to have the opportunity to nurture my child, but I am struggling with some of their learning and behavioral challenges. Lord, some days feel long and exhausting. Some days I feel we take one step forward and two steps back. I ask for strength and perseverance. Please equip me and give me patience. Please help me celebrate every step forward and recognize progress when it is made. Please help me see the wonderful attributes of my child Lord. I love my child for the following reasons Lord, *(pour out those reasons here)*. I thank you for the blessing you have given me and ask that you stand beside me while I shepherd them. Give me wisdom, as to whether or not I should seek outside assistance Lord. Please equip me, as I continue this journey alongside my child.

Amen

you are raising a special needs child

Psalm 127:3
Children are a gift from the Lord;
they are a reward from him. (NLT)

James 1:17
Every good gift and every perfect gift is from
above, coming down from the Father of lights,
with whom there is no variation or shadow due
to change. (ESV)

Psalm 139:13-14
You made all the delicate, inner parts of my body
and knit me together in my mother's womb. 14
Thank you for making me so wonderfully
complex! Your workmanship is marvelous—how
well I know it. (NLT)

John 9:1-3
Now as Jesus passed by, He saw a man who was
blind from birth. 2 And His disciples asked Him,
saying, "Rabbi, who sinned, this man or his
parents, that he was born blind?"
3 Jesus answered, "Neither this man nor his
parents sinned, but that the works of God
should be revealed in him. (NKJV)

your child is struggling

Lord,

I am a mom who is feeling helpless and brokenhearted as I watch my child struggle. Lord, I know I cannot fix every issue that arrives for my child, but I wish I could. I ask for wisdom on how to navigate this current struggle. I put my trust in you Lord, knowing that I cannot shield my child from their testimony. It is hard though Lord, but I know you use hard things to help us grow in you. Help me to guide my child and point them toward you during this time. Thank you that we are never alone in our struggles. Please help me to use this opportunity to point my child toward you Lord. Give me your wisdom and the right words when I speak my child. Help me to guide and disciple them in a way that brings them closer to you.

Amen

Hebrews 10:36
Patient endurance is what you need now,
so that you will continue to do God's will.
Then you will receive all that he has
promised. (NLT)

Psalm 138:8
The Lord will fulfill his purpose for me;
your steadfast love, O Lord, endures
forever.
Do not forsake the work of your hands.
(ESV)

Romans 5:3-5
And not only that, but we also glory in
tribulations, knowing that tribulation
produces [a]perseverance; 4 and
perseverance, [b]character; and character,
hope. 5 Now hope does not disappoint,
because the love of God has been poured
out in our hearts by the Holy Spirit who
was given to us. (NKJV)

you need outside help

Lord,
I know you have called me to be the
mother of my children but it has also
become clear I cannot not do it on my
own. Please guide me when choosing
assistance with the needs of my children,
help with the care of our home, and any
other support, which allows me to
breathe a little easier. Help me to still
stay engaged in what my child is doing,
even when we have outside support. Help
me to work alongside and appreciate
those assisting our family. Whether the
help is physical in nature or emotional
and spiritual through counseling, I know,
Lord, that needing help is not a sign of
weakness but rather it is my humbling
myself before you, knowing my
limitations, and ensuring success for my
child and family. Thank you for the
opportunity for others to pour into my
family.

Amen

you need outside help

Galatians 6:2
Share each other's burdens, and in this
way obey the law of Christ. (NLT)

Proverbs 15:22
Plans fail for lack of counsel,
but with many advisers they succeed.
(NIV)

Proverbs 12:15
The way of a fool is right in his own eyes,
but a wise man listens to advice. (ESV)

Proverbs 13:10
Pride leads to conflict;
those who take advice are wise. (NLT)

Lord,

Lately I am feeling unworthy. I feel like being a mom isn't as high of a calling as some other careers and callings in life. I know Lord this does not come from you though, as you have told us we are worthy. I also know my career path does not equate worthiness, nor do the success or failures of my child. Please help me to remember that my willingness to live for you and do your will matters much more than any career title. Lord, your word tells us that stewarding our children and raising them to be arrows is important, so while I may feel my job is unimportant some days I need to recognize that is a lie from the devil. Please help me to stay in your word and truth, knowing I am worthy because I am saved in you and your love is approval is all that matters.

Amen

you don't feel worthy

Ephesians 2:10
For we are God's handiwork, created in
Christ Jesus to do good works, which God
prepared in advance for us to do. (NIV)

Psalm 94:19
When doubts filled my mind,
your comfort gave me renewed hope and
cheer. (NLT)

Titus 3:5
Not by works of righteousness which we
have done, but according to His mercy He
saved us, through the washing of
regeneration and renewing of the Holy
Spirit. (NKJV)

Hebrews 4:14
This High Priest of ours understands our
weaknesses, for he faced all of the same
testings we do, yet he did not sin. 16 So let
us come boldly to the throne of our
gracious God. There we will receive his
mercy, and we will find grace to help us
when we need it most. (NLT)

you feel you aren't productive enough

Lord,

Today I felt nothing I set out to do was accomplished. I feel I was putting out endless fires with children, caring for needs, making food, and cleaning, on a never-ending rotation. Lord, I know the devil wants me to feel I have wasted my time and energy and to convince me that the tasks of today were not fruitful. I know this is a lie though Lord. You have called me to care for others and to nourish my family. You have called me to be a good steward of what you blessed us with, and that means cleaning up messes and tidying our home, even when it often becomes undone again. I know that while it may not look on the outside like I have checked many boxes or been productive today, that I am doing exactly what I have been called to do in this season. I know you see all the tasks, that are invisible to many. I thank you for this season of life and the ability to care for all you've given me.

Amen

you feel you aren't productive enough

Colossians 3:23-24
Whatever work you do, do it with all your heart. Do it for the Lord and not for men. 24 Remember that you will get your reward from the Lord. He will give you what you should receive. You are working for the Lord Christ. (NLV)

Ecclesiastes 4:4-6
Then I observed that most people are motivated to success because they envy their neighbors. But this, too, is meaningless—like chasing the wind. 5 "Fools fold their idle hands, leading them to ruin." 6 And yet, "Better to have one handful with quietness than two handfuls with hard work and chasing the wind." (NLT)

1 Timothy 5:8
But if anyone does not provide for his own, and especially for those of his household, he has denied the faith and is worse than an unbeliever. (NKJV)

Proverbs 31:27
She carefully watches everything in her household and suffers nothing from laziness. (NLV)

you are making decisions

Lord,
We are faced with some major decisions
right now. They are weighing heavy on my
heart and I am becoming afraid of making
the wrong choice. I feel the burden of
each choice for my child, and I know I
need to release this to you Lord. I ask that
you make our next steps clear. That you
will close doors we should not
walkthrough and that you will give us
peace if something we thought would be a
yes, should be a no. Please help me bring
all of my fears and decisions to you Lord
and not dwell with those around me. I ask
for your confidence and assurance, as me
move forward. I thank you for your
wisdom and guidance Lord.

Amen

you are making decisions

Proverbs 16:1-3
We can make our own plans,
but the Lord gives the right answer.
2 People may be pure in their own eyes,
but the Lord examines their motives.
3 Commit your actions to the Lord,
and your plans will succeed. (NLT)

Psalm 25:4
Show me the right path, O Lord;
point out the road for me to follow.
(NLT)

James 1:5
If any of you lacks wisdom, let him ask of
God, who gives to all liberally and
without reproach, and it will be given to
him. (NKJV)

1 John 5: 14-15
Now this is the confidence that we have
in Him, that if we ask anything according
to His will, He hears us. 15 And if we know
that He hears us, whatever we ask, we
know that we have the petitions that we
have asked of Him. (NKJV)

you are planning your family's vision

Lord,

I know you have called me to steward my children and I am so grateful for this opportunity. I want to be intentional and thoughtful as we plan our commitments and activities this school year. Please reveal to me the areas in which we should focus. Please help me create a vision for our family that focuses on you, on strengthen our family's connection, on activities which use my child's gifts and talents, and on the academics which nourish and grow our brains. Thank you for your wisdom.

Amen

you are planning your family's vision

Ephesians 5:15-17
So be careful how you live. Don't live like
fools, but like those who are wise. 16 Make
the most of every opportunity in these evil
days. 17 Don't act thoughtlessly, but
understand what the Lord wants you to
do. (NLT)

Proverbs 16:9
The heart of man plans his way,
but the Lord establishes his steps.
(ESV)

Proverbs 19:21
There are many plans in a man's heart, but
it is the Lord's plan that will stand. (NLV)

Jeremiah 29:11
For I know the plans I have for you,"
declares the Lord, "plans to prosper you
and not to harm you, plans to give you
hope and a future. (NIV)

for the beginning of the school year

Lord,

I thank you for this new school year and for the opportunity to teach and guide my children at home, whether they are home full time or not. Please help me to guide them in a way that honors you and reflects your love for us. Please help me to keep our focus on you each and every day. I ask that you give me wisdom each day but especially when we are faced with bumps in the road. Please remind me that curriculum and academic success is not more important than my child's heart. Please help my family grow in you and our relationships with each other. I thank you for allowing this to be a year of growth. Please bless the teachers and mentors in my child's life and help them to steward my child in a way that also honor's you Lord.

Amen

for the beginning of the school year

Proverbs 22:6
Train up a child in the way he should go,
[a]And when he is old he will not depart
from it. (NKJV)

Proverbs 37:23-24
The Lord directs the steps of the godly.
He delights in every detail of their lives.
24 Though they stumble, they will never
fall,
for the Lord holds them by the hand.
(NLT)

Lamentations 3:22-23
The steadfast love of the Lord never
ceases;
his mercies never come to an end;
23 they are new every morning;
great is your faithfulness. (ESV)

Psalm 25:5
Lead me by your truth and teach me,
for you are the God who saves me.
All day long I put my hope in you.
(NLT)

it is Thanksgiving

Lord,

I am so thankful for the gift of motherhood. While it can sometimes be challenging and bring frustration, I am thankful for this gift and that you equip me to carry out your will each day. Lord, thank you for your wisdom, your patience, your endurance, and your example of compassion. Please let me see the joy in motherhood, even on the difficult days. Please help our family celebrate of each other and recognize the specific ways we each benefit and bring life and joy to our family unit. Please help us honor you with thanksgiving and praise, not only during this time of year but all throughout.

Amen

it is Thanksgiving

Psalm 107:1
Give thanks to the Lord, for he is good;
his love endures forever. (NIV)

1 Thessalonians 5:16-18
Rejoice always, 17 pray continually, 18 give
thanks in all circumstances; for this is
God's will for you in Christ Jesus. (NIV)

1 Chronicles 16:34
Give thanks to the Lord, for he is good!
His faithful love endures forever. (NLT)

Hebrews 12:28
Therefore, since we are receiving a
kingdom that cannot be shaken, let us be
thankful. By it, we may serve God
acceptably, with reverence and awe. (CSB)

it is Christmas season

Lord,
As we enter the Christmas season, I thank you for the gift of motherhood. To share such a gift as Mary did is extraordinary. I am so thankful I do not have to do seek perfection in motherhood, as you sent a perfect son to free us from such a burden. Lord, help me to slow down during this celebratory season. Help me to focus on the light you brought to the world and help me to bring that light into my home. Please help my home reflect the love you have for us. Let my children see love like Jesus's in my actions and let us worship and focus on you Lord. Please let this be a time of spiritual growth and reflection in our home. Thank you Lord for bringing the light of you son to this dark world.

Amen

it is Christmas season

Luke 2:11
For there is born to you this day in the
city of David a Savior, who is Christ the
Lord. (NKJV)
(encouraged to read chapter 2 entirely)

John 8:12
Then Jesus spoke to them again, saying, "I
am the light of the world. He who follows
Me shall not walk in darkness, but have
the light of life." (NKJV)

Matthew 5:14-16
"You are the light of the world. A city that
is set on a hill cannot be hidden. 15 Nor do
they light a lamp and put it under a
basket, but on a lampstand, and it gives
light to all who are in the house. 16 Let
your light so shine before men, that they
may see your good works and glorify your
Father in heaven. (NKJV)

it is Valentine's

Lord,
This Valentine's Day I reflect on your love
for us. I am so thankful you love me
without condition. Help me to show the
same unconditional love to my children.
Please help me emulate your love while
shepherding my children. Please help me
to remember the grace you have bestowed
upon me and let me show that same grace
to my children. Please help me to show
your love through both words and deeds.
Thank you for your never-ending love.

Amen

1 Corinthians 13:4-7
Love is patient and kind. Love is not jealous or boastful or proud 5 or rude. It does not demand its own way. It is not irritable, and it keeps no record of being wronged. 6 It does not rejoice about injustice but rejoices whenever the truth wins out. 7 Love never gives up, never loses faith, is always hopeful, and endures through every circumstance. (NLT)

Romans 5:8
But God demonstrates His own love toward us, in that while we were still sinners, Christ died for us. (NKJV)

1 Corinthians 16:14
And do everything with love. (NLT)

Ephesians 5:2
And walk in love, as Christ also loved us and gave himself for us, a sacrificial and fragrant offering to God. (CSB)

Lord,

As we enter this season of hope, I think of the hope I had when each of my children were blessed to join our family. I thank you for the gift of motherhood. I thank you for equipping me to guide my children academically, emotionally, and spiritually. I pray I will give my children the same grace you have given me, and I pray I will honor your word by using it as a foundation for our home. I thank you for the ultimate sacrifice of your son, so my children and I can have eternal life with you.

Amen

it is Easter

John 3:16

For God loved the world in this way:[a] He
gave[b] his one and only Son, so that
everyone who believes in him will not
perish but have eternal life. (CSB)

1 Peter 1:3-4
All praise to God, the Father of our Lord
Jesus Christ. It is by his great mercy that
we have been born again, because God
raised Jesus Christ from the dead. Now we
live with great expectation, 4 and we have
a priceless inheritance—an inheritance
that is kept in heaven for you, pure and
undefiled, beyond the reach of change and
decay. (NLT)
(encouraged to read chapter 1 entirely)

Psalm 62:5-6
Rest in God alone, my soul,
for my hope comes from him.
6 He alone is my rock and my salvation,
my stronghold; I will not be shaken. (CSB)

the end of the school year

Lord,

I thank you for another school year. While it may have not been perfect, I know *(fill in: homeschool, private school, public school)* is the path you have called my family to follow. Please help us celebrate the little wins and the progress made. Please help us keep our eyes fixed on you and know that checking boxes and grades is not what ultimately pleases you. Please help us enter a time of rest and rejuvenation. I know, Lord, that you don't seek perfection, but rather for me to carry out what you have called our family to do. I thank you Lord for the educational opportunities our family is blessed with.

Amen

the end of the school year

Psalm 103:1-2
Let all that I am praise the Lord;
with my whole heart, I will praise his
holy name.
₂ Let all that I am praise the Lord;
may I never forget the good things he
does for me. (NLT)

Ephesians 2:8-9
For by grace you have been saved through
faith. And this is not your own doing; it is
the gift of God, ₉ not a result of works, so
that no one may boast. (ESV)

family's vision

Dear Mom,

Planning a vision for your family can be so fruitful. When first brainstorming your vision, write down the attributes you want your family to possess and the top three priorities you have for your family.

Pray about what God wants for your family in this season and then speak with your husband and ask him to do the same. Once you and your husband have prayed and discussed your vision, ask your children what they love about your family unit and what they wish could change. Remember to be good and open listeners during this time. Sometimes children say things that surprise us or hit a nerve, either way it is our job to dig deeper. Ask open ended questions and allow this to be a time of growth as a family.

Then, together, it is time to finalize your vision. You an use the questions on the next page to guide the process. I always recommend putting your vision, goals, and family verse in a place where your entire family can see it regularly.

Much love,
Jenna

planning your family's vision

- What are three words would you like others to use when they describe your family? Example: close, encouraging
- What are do you enjoy doing as a family?
- What do you wish we spent more time doing together?
- Is there something that is bothering you about how we currently spend our time?
- What does our family value?
- What are our family's top three priorities during this season?
- What individual goals do we each have and how can we support each other?
- What verse supports our family's vision?
- How should we handle disagreements and consequences during this season?
- What is one way we can improve our family's communication?
- What qualities do we want to instill in our children & what are some practical ways we can cultivate these qualities?

Our family's vision

Verse:

Top three attributes we will strive for as a family:

    1.

    2.

    3.

Top three priorities during this season:

    1.

    2.

    3.

A goal for our family is to . . .